Ghost Towns

by Sarah Parvis

Consultant: Troy Taylor
President of the American Ghost Society

BEARPORT PUBLISHING

New York, New York

Credits

Cover and Title Page, © Michael T. Sedam/CORBIS; 4–5, © Jack Fields/CORBIS; 6, © Michael T. Sedam/CORBIS; 7T, © The Granger Collection, New York; 7B, © Photograph by David (Doc) Roberts; 8, © Bob Landry/Time Life Pictures/Getty Images; 9T, © Rex Hardy Jr./Time Life Pictures/Getty Images; 9BL, © Peter Baxter/Shutterstock; 9BR, © Richard Cummins/SuperStock; 10, © Rob Crandall/Stock Connection Blue/Alamy; 11T, © Courtesy of Legends of America; 11BL, © David Samuel Robbins/CORBIS; 11BR, © age fotostock/SuperStock; 12, © David R. Frazier Photolibrary, Inc./Alamy; 13L, © James Gritz/Robert Harding Picture Library Ltd/Alamy; 13R, © Robert Shantz/Alamy; 13 Background, © Baloncici/Shutterstock; 14, © Amritaphotos/Alamy; 15T, © Mark E. Gibson/CORBIS; 15B, © Underwood Photo Archives/SuperStock; 16, © The Granger Collection, New York; 17, © The Granger Collection, New York; 18, © Crew Creative; 19T, © Nicholas Bird/Alamy; 19B, © Roger Ressmeyer/CORBIS; 20, © Helene Rogers/Alamy; 21T, © Carolynn Shelby Method 9/Alamy; 21B, © Mary Evans Picture Library/Alamy; 22, Courtesy of The Real Mary King's Close/Continuum; 23, © Gary Doak/Alamy; 24, © Walter Bibikow/Jon Arnold Images Ltd/Alamy; 25, © Stuart Dee/Photographer's Choice/Getty Images; 26, © Joe Sohm/Visions of America, LLC/Alamy; 27, © Danny Lehman/CORBIS; 32, © Jane McIlroy/Shutterstock.

Publisher: Kenn Goin
Editorial Director: Adam Siegel
Creative Director: Spencer Brinker
Design: Dawn Beard Creative
Photo Researcher: Beaura Kathy Ringrose

Library of Congress Cataloging-in-Publication Data

Parvis, Sarah E.
 Ghost towns / by Sarah Parvis.
     p. cm. — (Scary places)
 Includes bibliographical references and index.
 ISBN-13: 978-1-59716-577-8 (library bdg.)
 ISBN-10: 1-59716-577-8 (library bdg.)
 1. Haunted places—Juvenile literature. 2. Ghost towns—Juvenile literature. 3. Ghosts—Juvenile literature. I. Title.

 BF1461.P375 2008
 133.1'22—dc22

                           2007042400

For more information, write to Bearport Publishing Company, Inc., 101 Fifth Avenue, Suite 6R, New York, New York, 10003. Printed in the United States of America.

10 9 8 7 6 5 4 3 2 1

Contents

Ghost Towns

The houses are all empty. No cars crowd the streets. The only sound in many ghost towns is the whistle of the wind through broken buildings. Sometimes even the buildings have disappeared. Then only the **spirits** of the men and women who once lived there are left behind.

Where did all the people go? Were they wiped out by war? Driven out by disease? Or did the lack of jobs cause them to move away? The answers can be found in the dark histories of these communities that ended in odd or mysterious ways. In the 11 ghost towns in this book, you'll discover the world's toughest prison, a city buried in **ash**, and a **colony** that simply disappeared.

The Gold Rush Ghost

Bodie, California

In 1859, gold was discovered in Bodie, California. Thousands of people soon moved to the area. They were hoping to get rich quickly. By the 1940s, however, very little gold could still be found in Bodie. With no more work, the **miners** left, and the town shut down. One person, however, is still said to call Bodie her home.

Bodie, California

Bodie, Calilfornia, started with only 20 gold miners around 1861. By 1880, it was home to about 10,000 people. With more than 60 **saloons**, the town was famous for being wild. Robbers, gamblers, and gunfighters lived among miners and store owners. Some say that a murder occurred in Bodie almost every day.

Several hundred Chinese people also lived and worked in Bodie. One of them was a maid for the successful businessman James Stuart Cain. It is said that when Mrs. Cain fired her, the maid was so upset that she killed herself. Park rangers who now look after the **abandoned** town say that her spirit has never left.

One night a ranger's wife was sleeping at the J. S. Cain house. She suddenly woke, gasping for breath. When she opened her eyes, Cain's maid was sitting on top of her. Fighting to get away, the ranger's wife fell off the bed. When she looked up, the ghost was gone.

J. S. Cain house

Is Bodie **cursed**? Some visitors think so. After taking objects from the town, such as pebbles or pieces of wood, they claimed they started having terrible luck. Some had car accidents. Others lost their jobs. Many of these visitors rushed back to Bodie and returned the items, hoping to get rid of their bad luck.

Headless Charlie

Jerome, Arizona

Some miners struck it rich with gold. Others searched for silver. Beginning in the 1880s, miners in Jerome, Arizona, found their **fortune** in copper. More than $500 million worth of the metal was taken from the Jerome mines before they closed in 1953. Was it worth the price paid in miners' lives?

Jerome, Arizona

Mining is a dangerous business. Accidents, fires, explosions, cave-ins, and poisonous gases are common. In 1918, uncontrollable fires swept through the mining tunnels beneath Jerome. So underground mining was stopped. Instead, dynamite was used to blast open the ground to get the metal.

During World War II (1939–1945), the United States needed lots of copper to make engines, planes, ships, and wires. So miners were kept busy in Jerome. After the war, the need for copper dropped and the town slowly died. When Jerome's last copper mine closed in 1953, only 50 people were left.

Today, the 88 miles (142 km) of abandoned mining tunnels that run under the town can be spooky. In the darkness, people claim to have seen Headless Charlie. Charlie was a miner whose head was chopped off in a terrible accident. His body was never found. His spirit, however, is still said to haunt the dusty tunnels.

The Inn at Jerome is said to be home to a ghostly cat. Workers have felt it brush past them in the halls and have heard its meow. The cat even leaves the print of its body in the beds where it sleeps.

WARNING! DANGER! Abandoned mines are deadly! Don't get trapped! STAY OUT! STAY ALIVE!

A deserted mine in Jerome

A Spooky Sheriff

Bannack, Montana

From the 1860s to the 1890s, the area west of the Mississippi River was known as the Wild West. Gamblers and **criminals** lived alongside cowboys and miners in this part of the United States. To keep people safe, the towns needed good sheriffs. It wasn't always easy, however, to tell the good ones from the bad.

Bannack, Montana

In the summer of 1862, gold was found in a **creek** in Bannack, Montana. A year later the town had 3,000 people and more crime than it knew how to handle. The townspeople elected newcomer Henry Plummer as their sheriff. No one knew he had recently been in jail for murder.

Henry Plummer

After Plummer became sheriff, people were still being robbed. Crime in the town got worse. In just a few months, more than 100 people were murdered. Plummer was accused of being the leader of a gang of criminals. Although he was never proven guilty, Plummer was dragged to the **gallows** by angry townspeople and hanged in January 1864.

By the 1940s, there was no more gold left in Bannack. The few remaining people moved away. Yet Sheriff Plummer's ghost is said to remain. People have seen it lurking among the silent buildings. Perhaps he is trying to prove his **innocence**.

According to **legend**, Henry Plummer's grave was robbed around 1900. Two men were said to have stolen his head. They carried it back to the Bank Exchange Saloon. It remained there for several years until the building burned down.

Hidden Homes

Anasazi Cliff Dwellings, Mesa Verde National Park, Colorado

The western part of North America was home to Native Americans long before miners and cowboys moved in. The Anasazi (*ah*-nuh-SAH-zee) were an **ancient** people who were already living in the American Southwest 2,000 years ago. In the 1100s, they began building homes in the sides of high cliffs. Then suddenly, around 1300, they disappeared. Would anyone ever see their beautiful homes again?

Anasazi cliff dwellings

In 1888, two ranchers in Colorado were looking for cattle that had strayed from the herd. Instead of cows, however, they came upon an eerie sight.

Tucked into the cliffs above them were crumbling homes that had been built by the Anasazi. The buildings were made out of sandstone bricks. The most amazing one is called Cliff Palace. It includes more than 200 rooms and 23 underground kivas, or meeting rooms. Some believe that the site is **sacred**. Spirits of the Anasazi have been seen around the kivas.

When the cliff **dwellings** were discovered, the Anasazi hadn't lived in them for more than 500 years. What caused them to leave? They probably moved away because of **drought** or warfare with nearby tribes. Whatever the reason for their disappearance, no one lives in the cliffs now except scorpions, rattlesnakes, coyotes—and spirits from a time long past.

Cliff Palace

A kiva

Scientists found more than a thousand broken and burned bones in the Anasazi's abandoned buildings in New Mexico. Many of these bones were from humans. Some believe they belonged to Anasazi victims who were killed and eaten by enemies.

Phantom Prisoners

Alcatraz Island, San Francisco, California

Surrounded by the cold waters of San Francisco Bay, Alcatraz Island was the perfect place for a prison. Beginning in 1934, it was home to the toughest criminals in America. Nearly 30 years later, however, the cost of running Alcatraz had become too high. The prison was shut down in 1963. The ghosts of some criminals, however, may still be lurking in the abandoned prison.

Alcatraz Island

Alcatraz Island was opened for tours in 1973. Tour guides there tell visitors about the strict rules that broke even the toughest criminals. For example, prisoners could not talk for more than three minutes on most days. It is said that many **inmates** went insane from the deafening silence.

If prisoners broke the rules, they could be beaten. Some were chained to the walls of **dungeons**, where they were forced to stand from morning to night. Others were left in cold dark rooms without any clothes.

The spirits of these long-dead prisoners can still be heard today. Tour guides and visitors tell of strange banging that comes from empty hallways. Screams and moans echo from the dungeons. More than one security guard has followed the sound of running footsteps. However, all anyone ever finds are the dark empty cells of Alcatraz.

A prison cell at Alcatraz

Gangster Al Capone was imprisoned at Alcatraz in the 1930s. He used to hide in the shower room to practice playing the banjo. Guards say the sound of his songs can still be heard there today.

Al Capone

15

The Lost Colony

Roanoke Island, North Carolina

In 1587, around 115 English **settlers** arrived by ship at Roanoke (ROH-uh-nohk) Island. The small island is located off the coast of North Carolina. The settlers hoped to make a new home for themselves there. Within three years, however, all of them would disappear.

Settlers on Roanoke Island

The men, women, and children who reached Roanoke Island were tired and hungry from their long journey. They lacked basic supplies, such as food and tools. So the colony's governor, John White, sailed back to England to get them. He left behind his family, including his newborn granddaughter, Virginia.

Due to war, White was unable to return for several years. He finally came back to the colony on August 18, 1590—his granddaughter's third birthday. However, the island was **deserted**. All the houses had been taken down. Not a single person was found. Only one clue remained. The word *Croatoan* (*kroh*-uh-TOH-un) was carved on a fence post. It was the name of a local tribe. Yet why it was written there, no one knows.

White returned to England, never discovering what had happened to his family. To this day, the mystery of the lost colony has never been solved.

John White discovering the word *Croatoan*

Sir Richard Grenville, an English explorer, had stopped on Roanoke Island in 1586. He left 15 men there to claim it for England while he gathered more settlers. When John White arrived in 1587, he found the bones of one man. There was no sign of the others.

A Violent Volcano

Pompeii, Italy

How does Pompeii, a busy city of 20,000 people, become a ghost town overnight? It gets buried under ash and rocks from the massive **eruption** of a volcano. The disaster in Pompeii was so swift and deadly, many people didn't even have time to escape. They were simply trapped forever where they stood.

Mount Vesuvius erupting over Pompeii, Italy

On August 24, A.D. 79, people in the Roman city of Pompeii felt the earth shake. A huge burst of ash from Mount Vesuvius rose more than 12 miles (19 km) into the air. Every hour, nearly six inches (15.2 cm) of fiery rock and ash fell on the city. The roofs of many homes caved in. Poisonous gas from the volcano filled the air.

People ran for safety, but many could not escape. About 2,000 people died on that terrible day. The city remained buried under many feet of volcanic **debris**, untouched and forgotten for more than 1,500 years.

Pompeii was rediscovered in 1748. Since that time, many of the city's buildings and homes have been uncovered. Now, the millions of tourists who visit the city can imagine what life was like before tragedy struck.

Pompeii today

Over time, the bodies buried by the volcano **decayed**. Empty spaces in the shapes of the victims were left in the hardened ash. **Archaeologists** poured **plaster** into the spaces. When it dried, the hardened plaster looked just like the people of Pompeii at the moment of their deaths.

A victim of Mount Vesuvius

19

A Cursed Shipwreck

Llanelen, Wales

A plague is a deadly disease that spreads quickly from person to person. The **bubonic plague**, or Black Death, was one of the most famous disease outbreaks in history. In the middle of the 1300s, it swept across Europe and Asia, killing 75 million people. Unfortunately, there have been other outbreaks of the disease. Each one killed many people—and sometimes turned busy villages into ghost towns.

Victims of the bubonic plague being buried

In the mid-1600s, a ship sank in the freezing waters near Llanelen, Wales. Only a few crew members survived. After they crawled ashore, villagers tried to nurse them back to health. The sailors only got worse, however. It soon became clear they had the bubonic plague.

One by one, the villagers became sick and died. Soon, every human in the town was killed by the disease. Over time, the buildings fell apart, and the town of Llanelen slowly disappeared.

Today, just a few ancient stones from the buildings remain. The only other reminder of Llanelen is a mysterious lady in white. Some people say this ghostly woman sobs as she walks the land where the doomed town once stood. Perhaps she cries for her fellow townsfolk, who died as a result of their kindness to strangers.

Years after Llanelen became a ghost town, some stones from the old village were used to make a bridge. Local legend says that even touching the stones on the bridge will bring bad luck.

The City Below

Mary King's Close, Edinburgh, Scotland

Mary King's **Close** was once a crowded neighborhood of narrow alleyways in Edinburgh, Scotland. By the 1600s, the area had become filthy, run-down, and full of disease. So city leaders decided to get rid of the dirty neighborhood by building on top of it. Their plan created an eerie underground ghost city.

Mary King's Close

In 1753, builders in Edinburgh, Scotland, knocked down the top stories of the buildings in Mary King's Close. They used the bottom half of the old buildings to hold up a large new one. The once noisy and busy alleyways were left below in silence. The empty underground streets were not opened to the public again for more than 200 years.

Today, the most famous resident of Mary King's Close is known simply as Annie. She was a young girl who died from the bubonic plague in 1645. Annie's ghost was first seen by a Japanese **psychic** in 1992. In one of the tiny underground rooms, the psychic suddenly felt sick. As she tried to leave, she felt someone tug at her leg. She turned to see the ghost of a girl, dressed in rags. Her hair was long and dirty. Since then, other visitors have seen Annie. Many now bring gifts for the lost little girl.

Mary King's Close

Tour guides have seen shadows in the shapes of humans gliding around Mary King's Close. When the lightbulbs in the underground passages burn out, the guides go in pairs to fix them. They are too afraid to go alone.

Lost Temples of Stone

Angkor, Cambodia

The **Khmer** ruled much of Southeast Asia from the 800s to the 1400s. They built a huge capital city at Angkor, Cambodia. In 1431, the powerful Khmer were defeated by people from Thailand. As a result, they were forced to abandon the city of Angkor. For more than 400 years, the beautiful city remained hidden deep in the jungle.

Angkor, Cambodia

In 1860, French explorer Henri Mouhot stumbled upon the hidden city of Angkor. He was amazed by what he saw. Since the Khmer were a religious people, they had filled their city with huge, beautiful stone temples. One of them, Angkor Wat, is thought to be the largest religious building in the world.

Today, **monks** often travel to Angkor to pray. They believe that the spirits of people who once lived there remain. Some monks have reported seeing ghosts of princes and princesses walking through the stone halls and courtyards. Perhaps these royal ghosts continue to rule the city of stone.

When a French archaeologist first walked through the newly discovered city of Angkor, he felt as if he was being watched. Terrified, he looked up and saw huge faces looking down at him from all sides. These faces were giant stone sculptures carved into one of the temples.

Carved faces in Angkor

A Haunted Pyramid

Uxmal, Mexico

The Mayan people lived in a huge area now made up of Mexico, Belize, Guatemala, El Salvador, and Honduras. They thrived from A.D. 200 until 900. In some places they remained powerful until the 1500s. Without using machines or metal tools, the Maya built enormous cities. They created tall pyramids and beautiful temples. So why did their advanced civilization die out?

Pyramid of the Magician

In the early 1500s, the Spanish arrived in Mexico looking for gold. During their search, they killed many of the Mayan people. The Spanish also brought new diseases to the area, like smallpox. These spread quickly among the Maya, killing thousands more.

As a result of the Spanish invasion, the incredible cities of the Maya became ghost towns and were forgotten. Some would not be rediscovered for hundreds of years.

The ancient city of Uxmal (oosh-MAL) is one such ghost town. It is helping archaeologists learn about the Maya—including their practice of **human sacrifice**. Atop the stone Pyramid of the Magician in Uxmal, Mayan priests used to sacrifice human beings to honor their gods. The ghost of one Mayan priest still haunts Uxmal. When he's seen, he is dressed in his ceremonial robe and feathers. Visitors have spotted him atop the stone pyramid as if getting ready for another sacrifice.

Uxmal, Mexico

To perform their sacrifices, Mayan priests sometimes chopped off the heads of their victims. Other times, they used a stone knife to remove the beating heart from a living person. Then the priest would throw the body down to the ground from the top of the pyramid.

Ghost Towns

Alcatraz Island, San Francisco, California
The ghosts of criminals roam free in this prison.

Bannack, Montana
A sheriff hanged for being a criminal still haunts this town.

NORTH AMERICA

Bodie, California
The ghost of a maid haunts an abandoned gold-mining town.

Roanoke Island, North Carolina
Settlers disappeared from this spooky island, leaving behind a one-word clue.

Jerome, Arizona
A headless ghost haunts the scene of his mining accident.

Uxmal, Mexico
A Mayan priest reappears atop a pyramid used for human sacrifice.

Anasazi Cliff Dwellings, Mesa Verde National Park, Colorado
Spirits of Native Americans are seen in buildings that are hidden in cliffs.

SOUTH AMERICA

Atlantic Ocean

Pacific Ocean

Around the World

Mary King's Close, Edinburgh, Scotland

A plague victim haunts the abandoned alleys beneath Edinburgh.

Llanelen, Wales

The ghost of a woman in a white dress walks the grounds of this forgotten town.

Pompeii, Italy

About 2,000 people were buried when a volcano erupted.

Angkor, Cambodia

The ghosts of princes and princesses are seen among a city hidden in the jungle.

Arctic Ocean

ASIA

EUROPE

AFRICA

Indian Ocean

AUSTRALIA

Southern Ocean

ANTARCTICA

Glossary

abandoned (uh-BAN-duhnd) left empty; no longer used

ancient (AYN-shunt) very old

archaeologists (*ar*-kee-OL-uh-jists) scientists who learn about ancient times by studying things they dig up, such as old buildings, tools, and pottery

ash (ASH) tiny volcanic pieces of rock and minerals

bubonic plague (byoo-BON-ik PLAYG) a deadly disease that is spread by fleas and rodents such as rats

close (KLOHSS) a Scottish word for a narrow alley

colony (KOL-uh-nee) an area that has been settled by people from another country and is ruled by that country

creek (KREEK) a small stream

criminals (KRIM-uh-nuhlz) people who have broken the law

cursed (KURST) having unhappiness or bad luck

debris (duh-BREE) scattered pieces of something that has been destroyed

decayed (di-KAYD) rotted

deserted (di-ZUR-tid) left empty or alone

drought (DROUT) a long period with little or no rain

dungeons (DUHN-juhnz) dark prison cells, usually underground

dwellings (DWEL-ings) places where people live; homes

eruption (i-RUP-shun) the sending out of lava, ash, steam, and gas from a volcano

fortune (FOR-chuhn) a large amount of money

gallows (GAL-ohz) a wooden frame used to hang criminals

human sacrifice (HYOO-muhn SAK-ruh-fysse) killing another person as part of a ceremony or as an offering to a god

inmates (IN-mayts) prisoners

innocence (IN-uh-senss) being not guilty of a crime or wrongdoing

Khmer (kuh-MAIR) people born in Cambodia; they ruled much of Southeast Asia from the 800s to the 1400s

legend (LEJ-uhnd) a story handed down from long ago that is often based on some facts but cannot be proven true

miners (MINE-urz) people who dig for minerals underground

monks (MUHNGKS) men who have devoted their lives to God and are part of a religious community

plaster (PLASS-tur) a mixture of water and tiny bits of rock that hardens as it dries

psychic (SYE-kik) a person who can communicate with the spirits of dead people

sacred (SAY-krid) holy, religious

saloons (suh-LOONZ) places where people can buy and drink alcohol

settlers (SET-lurz) people who live and make a home in a new place

spirits (SPIHR-its) supernatural creatures, such as ghosts

Bibliography

Deem, James M. *Bodies from the Ash: Life and Death in Ancient Pompeii.* Boston: Houghton Mifflin (2005).

Hauck, Dennis William. *The International Directory of Haunted Places.* New York: Penguin Books (2000).

Lamar, Howard R. *The Reader's Encyclopedia of the American West.* New York: Crowell (1977).

Perl, Lila. *The Ancient Maya.* New York: Franklin Watts (2005).

Reader's Digest Editors. *Vanished Civilizations.* London: Reader's Digest Association (2002).

Westwood, Jennifer, ed. *The Atlas of Mysterious Places: The World's Unexplained Sacred Sites, Symbolic Landscapes, Ancient Cities, and Lost Lands.* New York: Grove Press (1987).

Read More

Barber, Nicola. *The Search for Lost Cities.* Austin, TX: Raintree Steck-Vaughn (1998).

Bial, Raymond. *Ghost Towns of the American West.* Boston: Houghton Mifflin (2001).

Hook, Jason. *Lost Cities.* Austin, TX: Raintree Steck-Vaughn (2003).

Stone, Lynn M. *Ghost Towns.* Vero Beach, FL: Rourke Publications (1993).

Tanaka, Shelley. *The Buried City of Pompeii.* New York: Hyperion (1997).

Learn More Online

To learn more about ghost towns, visit
www.bearportpublishing.com/ScaryPlaces

Index

About the Author

Sarah Parvis is a writer and editor in New York.
She lives in Brooklyn and loves ghost stories.